To: _____

From: _____

Date: _____

The giver's favorite maxim:

_____

_____

_____

The giver's maxim:

_____

_____

_____

A BEAUTIFUL GIFT FOR A

BEAUTIFUL SOUL SEEKER

THE KISS OF THE SOUL

BY

ANNE WIEN LYNN

Gotham Books

30 N Gould St.
Ste. 20820, Sheridan, WY 82801
https://gothambooksinc.com/

Phone: 1 (307) 464-7800

© 2024 *Anne Wien Lynn*. All rights reserved.

No part of this book may be reproduced, stored in a retrieval system, or transmitted by any means without the written permission of the author.

Published by Gotham Books (February 28, 2024)

ISBN: 979-8-88775-657-8 (P)
ISBN: 979-8-88775-658-5 (E)

Because of the dynamic nature of the Internet, any web addresses or links contained in this book may have changed since publication and may no longer be valid.

The views expressed in this work are solely those of the author and do not necessarily reflect the views of the publisher, and the publisher hereby disclaims any responsibility for them.

CONTENTS

Chapter 1
Life and Value..1

Chapter 2
True Love and Soul Mate.. 40

Chapter 3
Life and Death, Body and Soul 107

Chapter 4
Big Love 164

Chapter 5
Music 182

Chapter 6
Mindset... 218

Chapter 7
Inner Peace 247

Chapter 8
Money and Wealth 269

Chapter 9
Work, Struggle and Success.....................................286

Chapter 10
Education and Upbringing 301

Chapter 11
Meditation and Silence.. 315

Chapter 12
Peace and War.. 328

Chapter 13
Culture, Art and Cultivation 341

Chapter 14
Greed 353

Chapter 15
Beauty...363

Chapter 16
 Truth and Wisdom 372
Chapter 17
 Time 381
Chapter 18
 Dream and Genius 388
Chapter 19
 Home 395
Chapter 20
 God 401

Chapter 1

Life and Value

Jan. 1 — Day 1

1. You're not just an ordinary flower in a garden; you're an infinite garden in a beautiful flower.

Jan. 2   Day 2

2. The first duty in a man's life is to make other people feel that life is lovely and full of hope.

Jan. 3   Day 3

---

3. Breaking an egg from outside, that's food; breaking an egg from inside, that's life.

Jan. 4 — Day 4

4. Even if you're just an ordinary nail, you still can be shaped into an amazing artwork.

Jan. 5   Day 5

---

5. A wise man never wastes time, energy and wealth.

Jan. 6 Day 6

6. If you cannot understand the misfortunes of others, you will not understand your good fortune.

7. A real man knows self-improvement in adversity, and self-discipline in prosperity.

Jan. 8 — Day 8

8. Some journeys need no roads, only a willing heart.

Jan. 9   Day 9

9. Life is like a flute, it may have many holes and emptiness, but if you work on it carefully, it can play magical melodies.

Jan. 10   Day 10

---

10. Stay safe, stay healthy, so you can stay peaceful, stay free, and stay happy; so you can maintain confident, elegance and dignity.

11. It's outstanding to win a prize, it's better to win people's hearts, it's best to win the whole world; but it's great to win yourself, it's greater to win peace, and it's greatest to keep the peace within you, so no matter if you can win, you will never lose.

@ Van Cliburn Competition 2022 with Yunchan Lim

Jan. 12   Day 12

---

12. Measure your life not by possession, but by how many hearts you touched, how many smiles you created, and how much love you shared.

Jan. 13 — Day 13

13. Life is an art about balance of holding on and letting go.

14. If you haven't gotten the right one yet, it's probably because you haven't changed the wrong self yet.

Jan. 15   Day 15

---

15. Open the birdcage, let the bird fly away, and return the freedom to the birdcage.

16. There is no mistake, only lesson. When a person makes a mistake and does not correct it, which is a real mistake.

Jan. 17 — Day 17

17. Some things that people call music is actually just noise, some things that people call beauty is just eye-catching, some things that people call friendship is just business, and some things that people call love is just desire.

Jan. 18   Day 18

18. Nothing is more lamentable than a man's life is like a bustling masquerade, but makes his hearts feel lonelier at the end.

Jan. 19 — Day 19

19. No one is perfect, but it doesn't mean that you have to change yourself in someone else's way.

20. Don't let anybody tell you who you are, you have to decide that for yourself.

Jan. 21   Day 21

21. We live by the sun,
    We feel by the moon,
    We move by the stars,
    We eat from the earth,
    We drink from the rain,
    We breathe air,
    We live in all things,
    All things live in us.

22. Fine wine is for enjoyment, if pay a big bill to get drunk, not worth it.

Jan. 23 — Day 23

23. We never look good trying to make someone else look bad. The more we let go, the higher we rise.

Jan. 24 — Day 24

24. Eagle sometimes flies lower than chicken, but chicken can never fly as high as eagle.

25. When you feel lost, you need to bring yourself back to yourself.

26. You can become Coco Chanel, you can become Marie Curie, you can become J. K. Rowling. You can become Yujia Wang... You can become yourself, but not only someone's something.

Jan. 27 — Day 27

27. Do you have positive energy or negative energy?

Check out what your energy level is. When you appear, do you give people the feeling of peace,

warmth, friendliness, elegant, integrity and trust? Mother Teresa's energy is at level 700, Jesus is at 1000.

28. The richest person is not the one who has the most, but the one who gives and shares the most, and the one who touches the heart, moves the soul and lifts people the most.

Jan. 29 — Day 29

29. In your life, except what kind of person you want to be, everything else is for others to see.

Jan. 30 Day 30

30. Bullying someone who is weaker than yourself is a sign of cowardice.

Jan. 31 — Day 31

31. Great idea and excellent quality will never get old.

Feb. 1   Day 32

32. When the judgment is by appearance, the vision of the real value of human being is lost.

33. We hope to improve our lives through education, jobs, wealth, titles, marriage, relationships... but in reality, we've entangled with these appendants of life, and lost ourselves.

Feb. 3   Day 34

---

34. The deeper your roots, the higher your branches. Humble yourself, so you can grow greater than the world.

Feb. 4   Day 35

---

35. You don't need to buy famous brands; you can become a brand yourself.

36. It's not birth, family, race, nation, language, faith, mores, titles, fame, status, wealth, health, looking, age make people different, but only morality.

Chapter 2

True Love and
Soul Mate

Feb. 6   Day 37

---

1. If you cannot find me in the dark, you will never find me in the light. Souls know each other beyond sights.

2. Love and marriage are not transactions; they are not established by money, desire, material or blood relations.

Love is priceless; It is mutual respect, understanding, trust, care and cherishing;

Love is the mutual attraction of two souls and the union of two hearts, nothing can stop a true love.

Feb. 8   Day 39

3. When most people are searching for flowers or fruits among the branches, you are searching for the owner. You know that the owner will bring you to her secret garden.

Feb. 9 Day 40

4. I'm from Lyra. Are you a seed of inter-stars too? or a native old soul of the Earth? on a mission to save and rise other souls up? and looking for your soul family?

Feb. 10   Day 41

5. To those who know my soul,
   I'm everywhere.
   To those who know only my face,
   I'm just a stranger.

6. It's better to live with a soul mate rather than a roommate, so you won't feel homeless; it's better to stay alone with God rather than someone whom is godless, so you will never get lost.

Feb. 12 Day 43

7. When your love becomes your soul, your soul becomes your love.

Feb. 13   Day 44

8. May all who love each other will be always together; may all who are together will always love each other.

9. Valentine's Day is neither a Chocolate Day nor a Flower Day; it's a day to remind us if we truly love someone every day.

Feb. 15 — Day 46

10. The real kiss is when a soul meets its soul mate, it's the combination of two hearts.

11. We can never find a perfect love; we can create a true love.

Feb. 17 — Day 48

12. My face is not always available, my soul is.

13. If you cannot smell the fragrance of the soul, you will not find the way to enter the immortal garden of true love.

14. True love is only between two hearts. Trust and respect is the only thing worth living for.

15. If you want to be really powerful, peaceful, beautiful, happy, wise, even immortal, only one secret – to love God and someone with your full heart and whole soul.

16. Distance never kills a relationship; closeness never builds a relationship. It's the caring of one's feeling that builds faith and maintains a relationship.

17. Lust is an endless sea, can drown personality and conscience; Love is the infinite universe, can lift soul to be eternal.

18. If we are in each other all along, we are beyond time, we are beyond space, we are beyond words, we are beyond all languages.

Feb. 24 — Day 55

19. There is no distance between confidants, even if we are thousand miles or thousand years apart.

Feb. 25   Day 56

---

20. You're the song of my songs,
    You're the dream of my dreams,
    You're the heart of my heart.

Feb. 26 — Day 57

21. Sometimes, you even have no idea how should call the one you love the most, she/he's your baby, she/he's your God, she/he's everything, and she/he's everywhere. She/He's beyond all names.

It's better to live with a soulmate rather than a roommate, so you won't feel homeless; It's better to stay alone with God rather than someone whom is godless, so you will never get lost.

~ Anne Wien Lynn

Feb. 27 Day 58

22. The person you fell in love with at first sight is the one you recognized him/her with your soul. You both were in love in your previous life, so you could recognize him/her at a glance across thousand years.

23. Never say "Goodbye" to the one you love, even on your dying day. Say "Please take good care of yourself. I will come to meet you again in my next life, and I will still love you, ever forever."

24. On rainy days, even your shadow will leave you. But the true love will meet you in your mess, it will hold up an umbrella for you.

Mar. 2   Day 61

25. Those who are good at closing doors do not need locks and bolts, and no one can break in. True love does not require any ropes to bind, and no one can untie it.

Mar. 3 — Day 62

26. If you fall in love with a greedy person, you are likely to be betrayed. If a man is not satisfied with what he has, he will probably not be satisfied with what he will have.

27. To different people and different things, at the different time and different places, our EQ and IQ will be extremely different. Love can turn you into a god; also can turn you into a zero IQ baby.

Mar. 5   Day 64

28. From a fish to be a human, from a human to be an angle, the little mermaid had surpassed human's evolution of 100 million years in her short life.

29. True love can develop all potentials of a person, makes one extremely happy, free, intelligent and courageous, even immortal, because true love is from God.

Mar. 7 Day 66

---

30. True love has no enemy.

31. There will be never a delete key for true love.

Mar. 9 — Day 68

32. When you fall in love with someone, you can think about this vow first, even if you can't marry or live with the person you love.

"I will love, honor, and cherish you always. I will love you in sickness as in health, in poverty as in wealth, in sorrow as in joy, and will be true to you by God's grace, trusting in him, so long as we both shall live. I promise to love you above all others and to value you in my life as a precious gift."

Mar. 10 — Day 69

33. Everybody will pass away, but our souls and love will be forever. The song is ended, but the melody lingers on...

34. Love should be the waltz for two,
not the dying swan for one.

Mar. 12   Day 71

35. This is one of my favorite quotes on love: "A thousand half-loves must be forsaken to take one whole heart home. ——Rumi"

36. I can't promise to help you solve all your problems, but I can promise that I will never let you face everything alone.

Mar. 14   Day 73

---

37. True love and loyal friend are two of the hardest things to find.

Mar. 15 Day 74

38. The experience of love is often like a scene of sacrificing oneself to save other's life on the battlefield.

Mar. 16   Day 75

---

39. Love is what makes our every heartbeat.

40. About True Love, there are so many words in the dictionary are unnecessary, and there are many new words need to be invented.

Mar. 18   Day 77

---

41. A real man doesn't love the most beautiful girl in the world; he loves the one who makes his world the most beautiful.

Mar. 19   Day 78

---

42. Life is not about what we have, it's about who we have.

Mar. 20 — Day 79

43. The simplest tone requires the hardest practice, the place closest to you needs to take the longest journey.

Mar. 21   Day 80

44. To love is to turn love from a noun into a verb.

45. Sun is for days, moon is for nights, poem is for days and nights, music is for transcending time and space, love is for eternity.

46. True love can give you enough power to be loyal. Only true love can make a man understand the great love of God.

Mar. 24 　　　　　　　　　　　　　　Day 83

47. The most valuable possession you can own is true love for someone or something. The most powerful weapon you can be is an instrument of peace.

48. Only give the moments of your heaven to the one who is willing to hold your hand and walk with you through your hell.

49. Live with someone whom looks at your virtues with magnifier; live not with someone whom looks at your wrinkles and grey hairs with microscope.

Mar. 27   Day 86

---

50. The one who really love you may forget your age, but will never forget your birthday.

51. To love with soul. The combination of two bodies is short-lived; the union of two souls will be long lasting.

52. Princes, there were, there are, there will be, Beethoven is only one. Beautiful women, there were, there are, there will be, true love is only for one.

Mar. 30   Day 89

---

53. Love begins with removing all obstacles that prevent you to love.

Mar. 31 — Day 90

54. Are you looking for or living with a life partner or a soul mate? Congratulations if the answer is 2 in 1.

55. Nothing can measure true love.

56. True love has everything except age, limit and death.

Apr. 3 — Day 93

57. True love can fill your whole heart, whole body, whole soul, whole life and whole world.

Apr. 4 — Day 94

58. Love does not give a person the right to possess, but rather respects, protects, supports and gives freedom to the person you love to be what he/she dreams to be.

59. There is a relationship more intimate than many marriages, it transcends time and space, and that is the union of two souls.

60. Seeking for true love? It's not outside you, its' right inside you.

61. International Music Competitions are primarily for business opportunities. True geniuses and masters don't need to participate in competitions, because it's not competitions that make them become geniuses and masters, but the true love for music. The great musicians play for touching people's hearts, for lifting all souls, they play for the whole world, not for the prize.

62. Either regain love, or regain freedom. Just don't waste the worth of your instrument and yourself.

63. When love becomes a beauty pageant, we have to talk about true love.

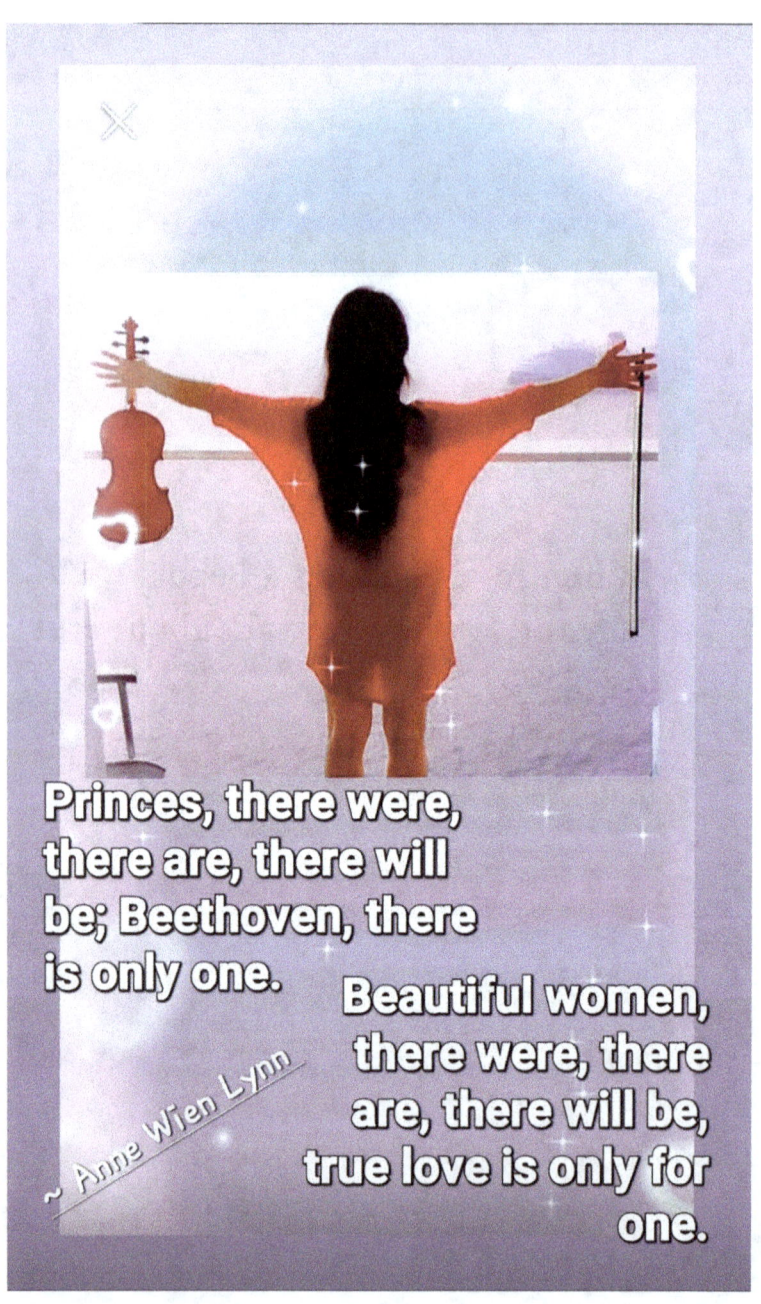

CHAPTER 3

Life and Death, Body and Soul

Apr. 10   Day 100

1. Many people like to collect, some collect gold and jewelry, some collect art works, some collect books, some collect old photos, some collect souvenirs, some collect beautiful women. I have always collected great maxims, because I can always bring them within me, and grow my soul every day.

Apr. 11 — Day 101

2. The death of flesh is not the greatest loss in life. The greatest loss is what dies inside us while we live.

Apr. 12   Day 102

3. **The ID for going to heaven is not our pretty faces, but our beautiful souls.**

Apr. 13 — Day 103

4. Don't read any famous book as a Bible, even a Bible, because every body's experience and understanding are different;

Only those words, people and things that can really convince you, move your heart and lift your soul are your Bible.

5. We feed our bodies everyday with food, how shall we feed and lift our souls everyday without reading, thinking, music, art, innovation, meditation, prayers, love and God?

Apr. 15 — Day 105

6. I'm just a visitor of this planet, to grow my soul, to know the secrets that lie beyond the world.

Apr. 16 — Day 106

7. Don't only trust your body, let your body trust you too.

Apr. 17 — Day 107

8. I've known many people's faces, but never known their souls; I've known many people's souls, but never seen their faces.

Apr. 18   Day 108

---

9. Don't judge people by their cars, look at the way how they drive and park.

10. May your soul is touched everyday by beautiful music, great thought, kind people and your own integrity.

11. The funeral of the flesh should become the wedding of the soul and eternity.

Apr. 21   Day 111

12. Your eyes don't recognize me; I'm the source of the sight of soul.

13. Any true relationship is about heart to heart, soul to soul.

Apr. 23   Day 113

---

14. My soul runs too fast, and I have no time wait for followers. I'm a follower of Rumi after him 800 years, and I'm behind Lao Tuz 2,500 years!

Apr. 24 — Day 114

15. "If you don't mind, may I ask how old you are?"

"I don't mind, if you don't mind my answer – My body: 100 years old; my heart: very very young; and my soul: over 2,000 years old. By the way, would you mind to tell me how young you are?"

Apr. 25   Day 115

16. Why does somebody think that when a person closes eyes, he must be asleep, and when a person's eyes are open, he must be awake?

17. Feng Shui not only affects the inside and outside of the building and our surrounding environment, the pattern of a person's INNER Feng Shui also affects and determines his luck.

18. Qin Shi Huang wanted to live forever, and built a huge imperial mausoleum to preserve his body; Jesus only lived 33 years old, and 3 days after his death, he left his tomb.

Apr. 28   Day 118

---

19. A reader who has read a thousand books has lived over a thousand times; a writer who has million readers has lived over million times.

20. A loser is one who failed without fighting. A hero is one who is destroyed but never defeated.

21. I admire kind people more than intelligent people.

May 1   Day 121

---

22. Are you seeking for beautiful face or beautiful soul? They are two big different levels. You show your level and your worth by what you seek.

May 2   Day 122

23. If there is no dignity in living, what is there to be joyous about? If there is dignity in dying, why should we be sad about it?

May 3 — Day 123

24. No matter how beautiful the scenery is, it will pass away, what can stay is life; No matter how beautiful a life is, it will pass away, only true love and great soul will be immortal.

May 4   Day 124

25. A person who wants to seek health and longevity without moral and spiritual growth can never achieve it.

May 5 — Day 125

26. Raging fire tests real gold, adversity and temptation test one's soul.

27. When a man's mind and character slumber, he only can see other's looks.

28. To be a beautiful song, let everyone listen to you like music; to be a great story, let everyone read you like a book.

May 8   Day 128

---

29. When you sigh: "I'm getting old." You should actually say: "Thanks God, I'm so lucky!" because there were so many young people past away unfortunately before they grew old...

30. To someone, death is the commencement of immortality.

May 10   Day 130

---

31. It's never time that can truly heal a person, but love, hope, faith and wisdom.

32. From sea to sky is a process of sublimation and transcendence, which is from tangible to intangible, from heart to soul, from finite to eternal.

33. The moment we love or we deceive is the moment we rewrite the chemistry of our bodies.

34. Some people have never met each other, but their hearts are always together. Some people live together, but they have never known each other.

May 14   Day 134

---

35. One thing cannot be acceptable in my life – my soul stops growing, just like those who have long stopped studying, reading and self education. No, my soul, stops sleeping, let's grow up, let's fly.

May 15   Day 135

36. Ordinary people go through 4 steps of life – birth, growth, aging and death. Great souls are birth and growth – grow to heaven, grow to immortality.

37. Some people only communicate with those who are around them, some people communicate with those who lived thousand years ago and those who live thousand years later.

38. The meaning of a body's existence is to give birth to a soul; the meaning of the soul is to find the secret of transcending the world and grow into immortality.

39. Some small men live in big bodies. Some great men live in small bodies.

40. Alive, be a man of men; dead, be a soul of souls.

May 20   Day 140

41. The body will grow old, but the soul can grow infinitely.

42. Birth and death depend on God. Everything has the karma. Therefore, wise men fear not the death of body, but the death of soul.

May 22   Day 142

---

43. Although time has left mottled noises, it did not prevent the masters' expressions across time and space from touching our hearts.

May 23   Day 143

---

44. A wise man is not getting older, but growing more mature.

May 24 · Day 144

45. A man who has an excellent mind and a great soul is nobler than a king.

46. Everybody is a soul, and every heart is my temple.

May 26   Day 146

---

47. If you learned the secret of the immortality of the soul, if you understood the wisdom of how to transcend this world, you would not fear the death of flesh.

May 27   Day 147

---

48. There are some things we will never lose; even Grim Reaper cannot touch love, truth, inner peace, real beauty and immortal souls...

49. Someone is alive, but he's been already dead; someone is dead, but still has been alive.

May 29 — Day 149

50. I'm not here (inside the tomb), I'm everywhere, I'm right within you, and forever love you.

May 30   Day 150

---

51. Judge not by a person's success or failure. Someone even can rise again from the death. @ Easter.

May 31   Day 151

---

52. If you're helping someone and expecting something in return, you're doing business, not kindness.

Jun. 1 — Day 152

53. Wherever you go, be the soul of any place.

Jun. 2   Day 153

54. People complain about the outside world, a lot of it is because they are escaping their inner growth.

Chapter 4

Big Love

Jun. 3　　　　　　　　　　　　　　　Day 154

---

1. Let's always pray for those who cannot pray for themselves.

2. When the power of love overwhelms the love of power, the world will know peace.

Jun. 5 — Day 156

3. Only by loving all sentient beings can a man understand the big love of God, can also understand the truth of harmony between mankind and nature.

Jun. 6   Day 157

---

4. The word Animal is derived from the ancient Greek word Anima; it means Soul and Life. All anima can feel music and love.

Jun. 7 — Day 158

5. To be a real vegan is not only to stop eating meat, but also to stop harming any living being, stop taking anything that doesn't belong to you.

Jun. 8 — Day 159

6. Release lives, protect yourself with mercy.

---@ Vegetarianism and Karma

Jun. 9 — Day 160

7. Prayer, the world's greatest wireless connection and love. Thank you all who always pray for others, for strangers, and for world peace! God bless you all!!!

Jun. 10 — Day 161

8. For what I love, I have no time to die.

Jun. 11   Day 162

---

9. Love is the best medicine. If we lost love, no one could be saved.

Jun. 12 — Day 163

10. A person without love will not grow completely. Only love can inspire and unlock the potential of our lives.

Jun. 13 — Day 164

11. We can always pray for others when we are unable to help them.

Jun. 14 — Day 165

12. Everyone is struggling in life, so, be kind to others, and it's the way how we change the world.

13. **Humanity is greater than status.**

14. Keep the light of your heart on, it may lead others out of the darkness.

Jun. 17   Day 168

___

15. When sin got on a ride of kindness, I hope that would be a journey of redemption.

16. A happy childhood can heal a lifetime, an unfortunate childhood needs to take a whole lifetime to be healed.

Chapter 5

Music

1. Music education is not just the education of musicians, but also the education of man — the education of beauty, peace and elegance, the education of harmony, wisdom and nobility.

Jun. 20   Day 171

2. I'm not sure if "A woman who doesn't wear perfume has no future." But I'm sure that every lady who loves classical music has a special elegant fragrance.

Jun. 21 — Day 172

3. Raise our music, not voice. It is rain that grows the flowers of our souls, not thunder.

4. Behind every beautiful and great piece of music, there are some touching stories, there is philosophy and divinity. If we only play or listen to the note, we won't really understand music. Music is the language of the soul. Music is life.

Jun. 23 — Day 174

5. When we make music, the whole world is ready to listen, because everything in the universe needs wings to fly.

Jun. 24 — Day 175

6. Music is not what I do, it's who I am.

Jun. 25 — Day 176

7. Sometimes, music is more powerful than any words; sometimes, silence is more powerful than any voice. That's why good musicians and wise men know how to make a rightly timed pause.

Jun. 26 — Day 177

8. Music bonds people. Those who love classical music have a special temperament that makes them attracted to each other, even when there is no music or any instrument, even between strangers.

Jun. 27 — Day 178

9. Music links the world, music links all hearts, music is international language. Give a violin to every soldier, replace their guns, then the world will be more peaceful, beautiful and harmonious.

Jun. 28   Day 179

10. The universe has music for those who will listen. The world has truth for those who will seek.

Jun. 29 — Day 180

11. You're your best music instrument. Develop yourself, and then, sing.

Jun. 30 — Day 181

12. On the piano, if you played wrong key, you may practice again. But on the road of life, you have to recognize clearly the white and the black.

13. If mathematics, physics, chemistry and logic can nourish the brain, if literature and art can also nourish the heart and soul, then music can nourish everything, the whole world.

14. What the ear can hear is sound, but music is sensed by the heart. Music is the resonance of the soul.

15. Music embodies upbringing. Each instrument is a living art work, carrying the history, civilization, beauty and soul of human.

Jul. 4   Day 185

16. It's as if human doesn't eat singing birds, if aliens who are more powerful than human decide not to eat human, that will not be because human has powerful weapons, but must be because human has great music.

17. Music and poetry can shape an elegant appearance and build a wonderful soul.

Jul. 6   Day 187

---

18. The flute is not totally empty. It's the soul that flows through ... sings and flies. To be empty is not emptiness.

19. All the masters of classical music used A=432 Hz. If 432 Hz is the frequency of the universe, shall we tune the world back to 432 Hz?

Jul. 8   Day 189

---

20. Music is the most beautiful language, and language can also be as beautiful as music.

Jul. 9 — Day 190

21. Music is enough for a lifetime; a lifetime is not enough for music. A true love is enough for a lifetime; a lifetime is not enough for a true love.

22. To be like a musician, send beautiful music to the world, send harmony, love, peace, prayer and hope to the world. What we sent out will come back around. This is called karma.

Jul. 11　　　　　　　　　　　　Day 192

---

23. Love classical music, because love elegance. I've never seen elegance go out of style. Elegance is the beauty that never fades.

24. Music is an angel of interstellar in universe, it can connect everything.

Jul. 13   Day 194

25. One of our human dreams: Everyone should learn music, no matter what age, even if it's before birth, or after 100 years old; everyone should learn how to play at least one instrument, everyone should join a choir, and at least, everyone should sing every day. In this way, the world will become more healthy, peaceful, harmonious and beautiful.

26. I wandered to Greece,

   looked for the Lyre of Venus;
I wandered to China,

   listened to a millennium Guqin;
I wandered to Persia,

   borrowed a Reed Flute from Rumi;
I wandered to Italy,

   gave David a Stradivari.

   I came back home, and hands empty,
I heard God said to me:
"Music is right inside of you,
you're your best instrument."

Jul. 15 — Day 196

27. Every country is different, but when we make music together, the whole world is one family.

28. If I were a mother, I would form my family to be a choir; If I were a teacher, I would build my school to be a choir;

If I were a manager, I would build my company to be a choir.

If I were a priest, I would build my church to be a choir;

If I were a general, I would build my army to be a choir;

If I were a president, I would build my country to be a choir; If I were God, I would create the world – the whole universe to be a choir.

Jul. 17　　　　　　　　　　　Day 198

---

29. One of the greatest moments in our lives is when there is no music or any instrument around us, we can make music by ourselves.

30. After many years, when you finally understood a piece of music, a painting, a novel, a movie, a maxim, a person, what you understood was actually life.

Jul. 19 — Day 200

31. Every instrument is waiting for a great player; everybody is waiting for a beautiful soul.

32. In the music, there is all beauty. All beautiful music is for plucking the heartstrings.

33. It takes 3 years to learn speaking, 10 years to learn shutting up, a whole life to learn music, 1000s years to learn listening.

Music is enough for a lifetime, a lifetime is not enough for music.

A true love is enough for a lifetime, a lifetime is not enough for a true love.

~ Anne Wien Lynn

Chapter 6

Mindset

Jul. 22 — Day 203

1. Train your mind to be calm in every situation. Never lose inner peace or be controlled by anything even if the whole world seems upset, then you will know the secret on how to exceed the world.

Jul. 23 — Day 204

2. Tears do not prove the seriousness of a matter. The one who cried the loudest may not be the saddest one. When face the same situation, someone may laugh, and someone may keep silence with inner peace.

Jul. 24   Day 205

---

3. Keep two things on your lips every day, silence and smile, you will see the big difference.

Jul. 25   Day 206

4. As a leader, first of all, you need self-control, no matter what happens, never lose your temper, always maintain a calm and clear mind, and then you can control any situation, and lead your team.

Jul. 26 — Day 207

5. You can change your mind in a moment, and this moment can also change your life.

Jul. 27   Day 208

6. Unfortunately, people always fight because of misunderstanding, "ask a question" is always misunderstood as "reproach".

Jul. 28 — Day 209

7. People are so angry that sometimes they even forget the reason why they're angry.

8. Freedom is not the absence of control, freedom is everything under control.

Jul. 30 — Day 211

9. Remember what Buddha said:" I'm not what you think I am, you are what you think I am."

Jul. 31 — Day 212

10. Life is 10% what happens to you, and 90% how you react to it.

Aug. 1   Day 213

---

11. Moderation is the golden rule of happiness.

12. We become what we think about.
    Energy flows where attention goes.

Aug. 3   Day 215

---

13. Your mind is a garden, your thoughts are seeds. You can grow flowers, or you can grow weeds.

Aug. 4 — Day 216

14. There is nothing either "good" or "bad", only you think so.

Aug. 5   Day 217

15. A lamp can light up a room that has been dark for a thousand years.

Aug. 6 — Day 218

16. Sometimes, we need to move backward before we can move forward.

Aug. 7 — Day 219

17. Our mind is a mirror, adjust it, to see a better world.

Aug. 8 — Day 220

18. Nothing is unclean in itself, only if someone thinks something as unclean, then for him it is unclean.

Aug. 9   Day 221

---

19. There is only one step between heaven and hell.

Aug. 10 — Day 222

20. You can change your world with your smile, but don't let the world change your smile.

Aug. 11   Day 223

21. There are still many people in the world don't know how powerful the energy of mind (Psychokinesis) is. Different thoughts generate and radiate different biological energy fields. Mercy, love, prayer for others will generate positive energy and bring harmony and peace to the world. Greed, jealousy, lies, slander, hatred, discrimination, bullying, violence in mind, violence in words, violence in behavior can greatly affect our environment and climate, bringing different disasters. That's why wise people always control their minds, and always pray for world peace. Let's take good care of our minds.

                      ---@ Telekinesis

Aug. 12 — Day 224

22. Distance blocks nothing, ego closes everything.

Aug. 13 — Day 225

23. Keep a positive and peaceful mind. You are not responsible for other's negativity.

Aug. 14 — Day 226

24. There are so many stories in our lives happened in our minds, in our imaginations, in our dreams, and in our hearts, only half happened in reality. Take good care of our minds and our hearts.

Aug. 15   Day 227

25. You're not your resume, you're your current minds, God is watching.

Aug. 16   Day 228

---

26. What you think, you become. Your life depends on the quality of your soul.

Chapter 7

Inner Peace

Aug. 17   Day 229

---

1. To find peace, sometimes you have to be willing to lose your connection with some people, places, memories, things that make all noises in your life.

Aug. 18 — Day 230

2. I divide people in the world into two kinds, not man and woman, but those who have peaceful minds and those who have no peace in their hearts.

Aug. 19   Day 231

---

3. Be quiet, be the beautiful music, leave a peaceful space to others. Noise is the enemy of our souls.

Aug. 20   Day 232

---

4. **Victory is not about winning fights, it's about winning peace and inner peace.**

Aug. 21   Day 233

5. In our minds, we're all travelers of time and space, only the one who finds his inner peace can achieve the ultimate goal.

6. Maturity is a journey from a disturbed mind to a peaceful heart.

Aug. 23   Day 235

---

7. Only a peaceful heart can see a beautiful world.

Aug. 24 — Day 236

8. A peaceful heart does not mean a silent mouth; a silent mouth does not mean a peaceful heart.

Aug. 25   Day 237

9. One's top training is emotion stability; One's highest cultivation is inner peace; One's greatest wisdom is to walk with God, and give the world peace, love and harmony.

Aug. 26 — Day 238

10. Anger hurts the liver, horror hurts the kidneys, sadness hurts the lungs, over-thinking and anxiety hurts the spleen and stomach, ecstasy hurts the heart. Mercy and inner peace are the most beneficial for health.

Aug. 27   Day 239

11. The only right thing you always need within you is inner peace. A heart at peace gives wisdom to the mind and life to the body.

Aug. 28 — Day 240

12. My only wish for myself and for everyone is to have a peaceful heart.

Aug. 29 — Day 241

13. Nothing can take your peace of mind away unless you allow it.

Aug. 30   Day 242

---

14. Keep a peaceful mind, and always leave a quiet space for people around you to work, study, rest, think, listen to the music, sleep, meditate, pray…

Aug. 31   Day 243

15. Though we seem to be sleeping, there is still a spirit that directs us to be a nice one, a better one, a greater one and a peace maker in our dreams.

Sep. 1   Day 244

---

16. Expectation is the root of all heart aches. The secret of a peaceful heart is to love all beings, and never expect or ask for any return.

17. Inner Peace is a silence but super powerful energy from the wisdom of God.

18. At a quiet place in your heart, you can communicate with some great souls, with God, with nature, and with yourself.

Sep. 4   Day 247

19. True happiness comes from inner peace; true inner peace comes from the confidence and the faith in God.

Sep. 5   Day 248

---

20. To be absent from drama is to be present with peace.

CHAPTER 8

Money and Wealth

Sep. 6   Day 249

1. Money is meant to be used, human are meant to be loved. But the world seems to have turned upside down, and this is the source of so many tragedies.

Sep. 7 — Day 250

2. Money is maybe the shell of something, but not the kernel; Money can bring you food, but not appetite;

Money can bring you medicine, but not health;

Money can bring you fine clothes, but not elegance;

Money can bring you a mansion, but not a home;

Money can bring you acquaintances, but not friends; Money can bring you servants, but not loyalty;

Money can bring you women, but not love;

Money can bring you enjoyment, but not happiness; Money shows prices, but not value.

Sep. 8   Day 251

---

3. Pray for the things that money cannot buy;

   To be rich with the things that never lose value.

Sep. 9   Day 252

4. Money doesn't represent value, the way how we make and use money do.

Sep. 10 — Day 253

5. There is no waste in the world. The so-called waste is the wealth that has been misplaced.

Sep. 11 — Day 254

6. Is a person's dignity based on power and money?

Sep. 12 — Day 255

7. You can know the quality and the value of a man by what he spends time and money for.

8. There are two patterns in creating wealth - some people work for money, and some people let money work for them.

Sep. 14   Day 257

9. Are we truly rich? Let's count how much we have that money can't buy.
    1). Time
    2). Health
    3). Genuine relationships and Intimacy
    4). Character
    5). Emotional well-being and A Peaceful Mind
    6). Passion
    7). True Love
    8). True Happiness,
    9). True Friends
    10). Home (not a house)
    11). Morality
    12). Heart of Appreciation
    13). Honesty, Trust and Loyalty
    14). Respect of Others
    15). Conscience
    16). Integrity
    17). Knowledge

18). Talent and Genius
19). Wisdom
20). Inner Beauty
21). Cultural Accomplishment
22). Politeness
23). Upbringing
24). Aesthetic taste and Elegance
25). Creativity

Sep. 15   Day 258

10. Many musicians and artists struggled with poverty during their lifetimes, but after their deaths we see the value of their works.

Sep. 16   Day 259

11. The greatest misfortune of mankind is to measure success with $$$, so the index of health, wisdom, happiness, and even morality all decline accordingly.

Sep. 17   Day 260

12. **Bad gains are truly losses.**

Sep. 18   Day 261

13. No matter how poor you are, keep the tinder. The real darkness is in a man's heart.

14. Your age doesn't prove your maturity. Your degree doesn't prove your education. Your appearance doesn't prove your upbringing. Your income doesn't prove your value. Your title doesn't prove who you are. Your soul and the way how you treat others do.

Chapter 9

Work, Struggle and Success

Sep. 20 — Day 263

1. If we do nothing, we may not encounter failure, but we will never encounter success.

Sep. 21   Day 264

---

2. If you don't love the job you do, no matter how much money you make, you will never reach success.

Sep. 22   Day 265

3. Success is not the most important thing, how to success and what it means is.

Sep. 23   Day 266

---

4. All great people had faced hard times.

Sep. 24   Day 267

5. It's good to applaud the winners, it's better to cheer for the losers, and it's best to win the applause yourself.

Sep. 25   Day 268

---

6. If you don't fight for what you want, don't cry for what you lose.

Sep. 26   Day 269

---

7. Be strong and move on, after the dark night and hard time, it's the time for you to shine again.

Sep. 27   Day 270

8. A winner is the one who never stop trying.

Sep. 28   Day 271
_____

9. Erase the traces of labor with labor.

Sep. 29 — Day 272

10. Footprints are only left on the muddy path.

Sep. 30   Day 273

---

11. If we don't plane for a miracle in our lives, we only can see the miracle in other's life.

Oct. 1   Day 274

---

12. Fame and fortune only have temptation; Common cause and love create cohesion.

Oct. 2   Day 275

13. If you don't make the time to work on creating the life you want, you're eventually going to be forced to spend a lot of time dealing with a life you don't want.

Chapter 10

Education and Upbringing

Oct. 3 — Day 276

1. Never close school inside you. The purpose of education is to teach young people how to educate themselves for their whole life. There are many people start their early education before going to school, even get prenatal education, and there are many seniors still learn new knowledge after retirement.

Oct. 4   Day 277

---

2. Every youth should read " Anna Karenina", "Notre Dame", "Madame Bovary", "The Lady of the Camellias", "Les Misérables", "Tess of the d'Urbervilles", "Rebecca", "The Scarlet Letter", "One Hundred Years of Solitude", "Othello", "The Piano", "Atonement" ... Because such classic tragedies are still happening in the world, everywhere, every day...

Oct. 5   Day 278

---

3. An impolite man is a partner of arrogant and ignorant;

A gentleman combines wisdom, courage and elegance in one.

Oct. 6 — Day 279

4. Just because you respect others doesn't mean that person is excellent, it means that you're excellent.

Oct. 7 — Day 280

5. A "man" and a "gentleman" are very different; it's as if a "woman" and a "lady" are two concepts.

6. Upbringing is not others ask of us, it's first about our demands on ourselves.

Oct. 9   Day 282

---

7. Every child is an artist until they're told: "You're not."

Oct. 10   Day 283

8. Understanding is deeper than knowledge. Everyone knows ABC, only a few people understand XYZ. Those who understand will never judge, and those who judge will never understand.

Oct. 11   Day 284

---

9. No education is complete without music, art, peace, love, respect and God. Educating the mind without educating the heart is no education at all.

Oct. 12 — Day 285

10. The best outfit is self-respect, solemnity, silence, smile, elegance, politeness and confidence.

Oct. 13 — Day 286

11. True education should not only teach young people knowledge, but also teach them culture and upbringing; it teaches them not only a subject or a skill, but also educate them about life, wisdom, love, peace, beauty and truth; not only teach them how to make money, but also how to create wealth; teach them not only about what the price is, but also what the value is. Education's not about teaching people how to get a diploma or a degree, it's about how to educate themselves throughout their whole lives.

Oct. 14   Day 287

12. Laugh not at other people's mistakes or misfortunes, for God may forgive a man's ignorance, but not our arrogance and ruthlessness.

Chapter 11

Meditation and Silence

Oct. 15 — Day 288

1. Meditation is the secret of all growth in spiritual life.

Oct. 16   Day 289

---

2. Meditation is not a destination, it's your passport.

Oct. 17 — Day 290

3. If you cannot understand my silence, you will not understand my words either. Sometimes, pauses and silences are also a part of music; meditation and prayer are also a part of life.

Oct. 18 — Day 291

4. Human body has many untapped potentials that can be obtained through meditation, zen, qigong, inner alchemy, yoga and chakra opening ...People can be divided into two levels – those who are controlled by natural instincts, and those who enter into the self-control of intelligent consciousness.

5. Meditation is not at the beautiful beach or in a zen room, you can bring it with you to be anywhere.

Oct. 20 — Day 293

6. Shallow waters are noisy, deep waters are silent.

Oct. 21   Day 294

---

7. Never assume that LOUD is strong and QUIET is weak.

8. Zen sitting is like a pyramid, which is the most stable shape.

Oct. 23   Day 296

9. When you meditate, completely relax your body, empty your mind, fully return to the natural state, resonate with the magnetic field of the universe, and your body will absorb the high-dimensional energy of the universe.

Oct. 24 — Day 297

10. Loneliness has been the experience of many great thinkers, writers, musicians, artists and scientists. Solitude can stimulate imagination and creative, can improve concentration, and can help self-healing and self-integration.

Oct. 25 — Day 298

11. Music and meaningful silence is better than meaningless words.

Chapter 12

Peace and War

Oct. 26 — Day 299

1. When music, art, culture, education, beauty, respect, love, peace, human rights and God are better understood, there will be no violence and war. And this is the lesson for every human lifelong learning.

Oct. 27   Day 300

---

2. Better than a thousand hollow words is one word that brings peace.

Oct. 28   Day 301

3. Humans need to learn Nonviolent Communication, and then we will have a more civilized world full of positive energy, understanding, respect, peace, love and creativity.

Oct. 29   Day 302

4. Many people learn kung fu, but many of them do not know what real kung fu is.

Kung Fu goes beyond losing and winning.

Kung Fu is about when to move forward or backward.

Kung Fu is self-control.

Kung Fu is the art of balance, the art of stopping war.

The real kung fu is about how to make peace with others, with oneself, and how to make harmony with the world.

Oct. 30   Day 303

---

5. All wars fought between brothers.

Oct. 31   Day 304

---

6. If you want to change your world to be peaceful, make peace with yourself first.

Nov. 1   Day 305

---

7. Power and tyranny have never conquered people's hearts.

Nov. 2   Day 306

8. Any form of violence -- including verbal violence and the violence in the minds -- is a disgrace to human civilization

Nov. 3 Day 307

9. Victory is not about winning fights, it's about winning peace and inner peace.

Nov. 4 — Day 308

10. One of the greatest Kung Fu and wisdoms in the world is how to find peace within you, and how to make your enemy to be your friend without fighting.

Nov. 5 — Day 309

11. Remember: During the 8 hours we work every day, we also have another job, a job of 24/7, a job inside us, named PEACE, and we work for the whole world.

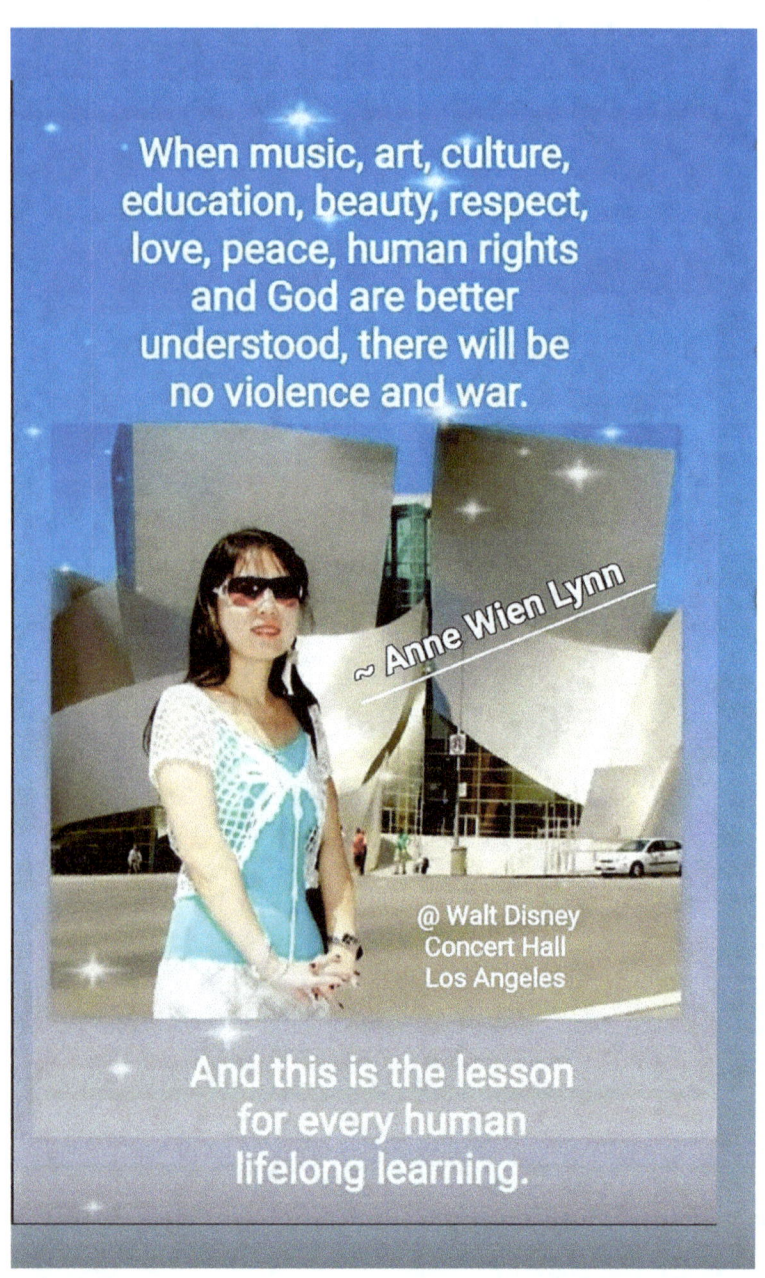

Chapter 13

Culture, Art and Cultivation

Nov. 6   Day 310

1. It is not mountains, rivers, oceans, countries, races, languages or religions that divide human beings. Music, art, beauty, love and all cultures have long connected people's hearts.

Nov. 7   Day 311

---

2. Let's learn these beautiful languages of the universe – Music, Love, Peace and Silence.

Nov. 8 — Day 312

3. No matter it's big or small, every city should have concert hall, theatre, art gallery, library, museum, stadium, cinema, church/temple/mosque, school, chorus and many artists... until it's no longer to need a prison.

Nov. 9 — Day 313

4. When we are learning a language, we will definitely find that we are actually learning a culture.

Nov. 10   Day 314

5. Masters are never made of copies.

6. Literary works are the spirit, cultivation and morality of a writer, and literature is the spirit, cultivation and morality of a nation and an era.

Nov. 12   Day 316

7. Don't confuse freedom with indulgence, our civilization once declined because of this.

Nov. 13   Day 317

8. A word can change a mind, a sentence can change a life, and a book can change the world.

Nov. 14 Day 318

9. It's good to read poems, it's better to become a poet, it's best to become a living poetry.

Nov. 15   Day 319

10. Art is how we decorate space, Music is how we decorate time, Morality is how we decorate ourselves, Love is how we decorate the world.

Chapter 14

Greed

Nov. 16   Day 320

---

1. God once walked with man in heaven. Man could get eternal life, but they were expelled from the paradise because of greed, envy, arrogance, ambition for power, and thus lost the wisdom of the way of eternal life.

Nov. 17 — Day 321

2. A greedy man always loses more than he gains, just like a generous man always gets more than he gives. The fruit is always much bigger than the seed. This causation is called KARMA.

Nov. 18   Day 322

3. If human beings do not control excessive desires, and maintain purity of body and mind, it will be difficult for medical research to treat and prevent the emergence of many new diseases.

Nov. 19   Day 323

4. With greed and hypocrisy as two legs, a man would never have an upright spine.

Nov. 20 — Day 324

5. Power or leadership is not an opportunity to satisfy personal desires and greed.

Nov. 21   Day 325

---

6. A greedy man will never be loyal to God nor to anyone.

Nov. 22   Day 326

_____

7. Greed and jealousy once caused angels to fall.

Nov. 23 Day 327

8. Greed and corruption are spiritual cancers of humans.

Chapter 15

Beauty

Nov. 24   Day 328

---

1. True beauty is not for attracting eyes, it's for moving hearts, and elevating souls.

Nov. 25   Day 329

2. A flashy appearance only attracts those eyes which love vanity.

Nov. 26   Day 330

3. There's no most beautiful woman in the world. Every woman has the most beautiful moment in her life and in her lover's eyes.

Nov. 27 — Day 331

4. Scenery belongs to those who enjoy it; Beauty belongs to those who discover and appreciate it.

Nov. 28   Day 332

---

5. Travel not only for the beautiful scenery in eyes, let's become eternal omnipresent scenery in people's hearts.

Nov. 29   Day 333

---

6. Good looks is unlikely express an educated lady, gorgeous dress cannot either create an excellent woman!

Nov. 30 — Day 334

7. The real beauty in the universe is seen with heart and soul, not with eyes. Eyes are useless when the heart is blind and the soul is sleeping.

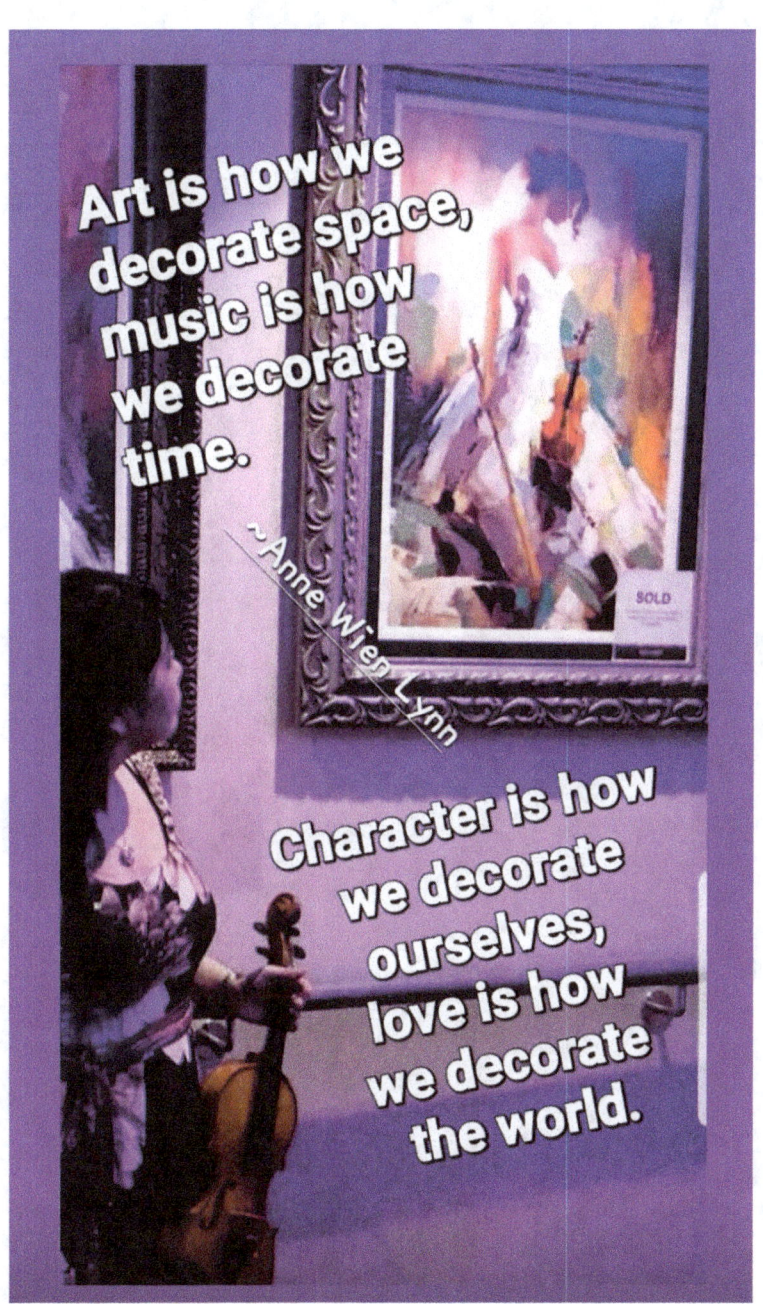

Chapter 16

Truth and Wisdom

Dec. 1 — Day 335

1. Heaven is not a destination to be found, but a place to be created. Without a beautiful heart, without inner peace, without love and great wisdom, we will never find heaven outside of us.

Dec. 2   Day 336

---

2. Some people like to learn methodology, but not truth; Methodology makes you smart, but truth gives you wisdom.

Dec. 3   Day 337

---

3. Nothing is so gentle as water,
nothing is so strong as water,
nothing is so strong as gentleness.

Dec. 4   Day 338

---

4. The place where you walk to the end of waters is the time that you sit down and watch the clouds rise up.

Dec. 5   Day 339

---

5. A half truth is a whole lie.

Dec. 6   Day 340

---

6. Be like water, soft, but never weak.

Dec. 7　　　　　　　　　　　　　　Day 341

7. Truth is not at the top of the pyramid, it is the cornerstone.

Chapter 17

Time

Dec. 8   Day 342

---

1. Every present moment can be the axis of life. To change the present is to change the past and the future of timeline. You don't have to dwell on one's past. The encounter of two people and the change of the present is a choice for the future. You are who you want to be.

Dec. 9   Day 343

---

2. Time is precious; make sure you spend it with right people and for the greatest goal.

Dec. 10   Day 344

3. Time is slow for those who wait, fast for those who enjoy, long for those who lament, short for those who celebrate; but for those who love, time is eternal...

Dec. 11   Day 345

4. What we really love to do, we always can find time and way to do.

Dec. 12 — Day 346

5. I'm alone, but no time to feel lonesome.

Chapter 18

Dream and Genius

Dec. 13   Day 347

---

1. All history is the history of thought and ideas. There is no great genius without great aspirations.

Dec. 14   Day 348

---

2. Dreams keep me awake.

Dec. 15 — Day 349

3. Give yourself a piece of blank paper, as big as you want, to write or draw something as if you were a child with a dream, so what would you do? How big is your dream? I built a cosmic philharmonic island on this piece of blank paper, also wrote its story and eternal dreams...

Dec. 16   Day 350

4. Make yourself to be a star, not only fan other's flames, let people sing and dance around your sparks too.

Dec. 17 — Day 351

5. Whatever you dream, you can achieve it. If there is no one laughs at your dream, your dream is too small. Whatever you imagine, you can create it. Everything is now proved was once only imagined.

Chapter 19

Home

Dec. 18   Day 352

---

1. Home is not a place, it's a feeling; life is not measured by ages, but by moments; heartbeats are not heard, but felt and shared.

Dec. 19 — Day 353

2. Live in the heart of somebody, and become the home of somebody's heart. This home will be much bigger, stronger, safer, warmer, lovelier, happier and more beautiful than all the big houses in the world or even royal palaces.

3. There are so many beautiful places in the world. A place with love is home. Home is always the world's greatest destination.

Dec. 21   Day 355

4. The happiest place in the world is not at Disney Kingdom, it's not on the luxury royal cruise ship, it's not in romantic Paris, it's not at any beautiful beaches. It's in the warm clean bed after all day hard work, it's in the taste of home food, it's in your garden that's full of flowers and fruits; it's in the heartbeats of a sweet kiss, it's in the loyal embrace at your weakest moments, it's at any place where you share love and peace with the world...

Dec. 22   Day 356

---

5. Home is where your heart is at peace.

Chapter 20

God

Dec. 23   Day 357
---

1. Be with God, not just cry out to Him in times of emergency.

2. A real religion doesn't teach people to build big churches, beautiful temples, or grand mosques; it builds the heart to be a church, the soul to be a temple, the prayer to be a mosque, and the love to be a priest. Therefore, God will always live within us.

3. Our relationship with God will determine all our other relationships.

Dec. 26   Day 360

4. Conscience is God's presence in man. Man cannot treat other lives like garbage, and worship God at the same time.

5. From a macro perspective, we are all microorganisms; from a micro perspective, we are all universe. In the eyes of God, we are all children; in the eyes of little kids, we are all gods.

6. Those who seek only for money, power, and beautiful faces without knowing God will never get true wealth, true power, true love and real beauty.

7. There is no top of the world until we reach God. We rise by lifting others.

8. A religion is not a true religion if it is not based on respect for life, it is not until man extends his compassion to all living beings that humanity can finally find peace.

Dec. 31   Day 365

9. If you can feel pain, you're alive; If you can feel other people's pain, you're a human being; If you can heal people's sufferings, you're an angel; If you can make people avoid sufferings, you're a god; If you can teach people how to avoid sufferings, you're God of gods.

Jan .1

Happy New Year!

May you grow faster and higher than the world, become an immortal great soul.

Your favorite maxim:

_____

_____

_____

Your own maxim:

_____

_____

_____

Date:

_____

The End

www.ingramcontent.com/pod-product-compliance
Lightning Source LLC
LaVergne TN
LVHW021955060526
838201LV00048B/1581